ISBN 978-0-578-80481-1

Blossoming Grace

Seeds of Meditation in the Garden of Becoming

Holly Knutson

This book is dedicated with love
to my always and forever
anam cara, Audrey...

Acknowledgments

There would be no *Blossoming Grace* without the amazing encouragement of so many of my friends and family and I thank you all...

Al Knutson, my husband – I thank you for listening to me read these writings over and over while I tried to get everything just right. I thank you for your enthusiasm and for loving me through all of this...

Becky Flansburg has been an invaluable resource of tireless and patient support (technical and otherwise), and I thank you so much...

Chelsey Johnson, who created the artwork on the cover and the illustrations found on the pages of this book, as well as preparing it for publishing, I thank you from the bottom of my heart...

Each and every one of you have made this dream of mine possible, and there are not enough thanks I can give for that!

Let me be a
channel of
Great Compassion

Let me be a source
of Enduring Grace

Let my life be an
embodiment of

Truth

Love

Beauty

and Courage...

As I stand in my
naked brokenness,

I ask to be clothed
in Truth, Love,
Beauty and
Courage

My heart answers,
Do you not know
that you are
already MADE of
these things?

I am whole, yet not
wholly recognized.

Sitting in my dark
corner of pain,

I glimpse a faint
glow coming from
inside;

That's joy! That's
peace! That's love!

It's all there, deep
within...

Let it shine in all
its fullness.

Let your SELF be
heard in all of
your raging,
sacred, profane
and beautiful
glory;

Let your SELF be
known deeply

And allow healing
to begin...

When even the
faintest warm
rays of Truth
touch immense
icebergs of shame,

They are melted
into the Sea of
Love.

My heart revels in the silent, steady pulse of the Presence of Love as I rest in its tender Blessedness...

Bells of gratitude ring through my life as I awaken to all that is precious, holy and authentic.

In solitude, I
remember who I
am

A blessed Child of
the Universe

Whole, complete
and vibrating with
Love

One with all who
wander onto my
path

Seeing through
false masks, deep
into limitless souls.

When today is too
much,

Rest...

Give the hours
some time to pass

Gather your
strength

Let your soul be
restored

Renew your vision
for a new set of
hours

Receive the gift of
a new day with
hope and promise.

Sometimes, I
wonder

Where is the Light?

Deep inside, I hear
the Voice say

The Light is
Within, Without,
Above, Below

Bathe in it

Thank it

And warm
yourself to Life.

Memories of who I
am;

Treasures to be
opened in my
heart

Songs to be sung
from my soul;

Awakened to the
purity of Love;

The Gift received
from The Source of
All Good

Given, to be
shared.

My history is not
Who I am;

Who I am is what I
make of my
history , to emerge
as my True Self.

In the quiet hours
of my life,

I listen for The
Voice

Of Love

Of Peace

Of Blessedness

And, it is heard...

So, that when the
noise arrives once
again, I am
strengthened and
still.

We are all pieces of
The Source of Love

The Holy Puzzle
that is God/Spirit

Let us arrange
ourselves in
harmony with all,

So that this Love
may be fully
expressed.

Excavating,
digging up,
mining;

This is the work of
the Soul

Casting away the
debris, the
unwanted, the
unworkable

Leaving only the
true treasure

That is you.

Why are you so
afraid of your own
goodness?

Is it because of the
lies you have
always believed,

The lies of the
world and of your
own mind?

Leave them behind
and turn your face
to a new reality,

That you are
created from Love
and have only
Love to give...

To all questions

There is only one anwer...

LOVE

At times, all it
takes is certain
words to be spoken
or thought, and I
am taken back to
shame, the dark
hole of
unworthiness,
diminishment of
Self. Deep, searing
pain overwhelms
as tears burn paths
down my face. In
that moment, I am
touched by Grace;
My heart warms,
and I am once
again healed.

*In great joy and in
deep grief*

*There is one
Constant;*

*Spirit meets us and
joins with us to
celebrate or
console,*

*And we are
whole...*

The heart
welcomes this fresh
new day

Full of gratitude
for another chance
to give and receive
Love in all its
forms

Breathe it in and
deeply know the
enormity of this
Gift.

Connection with
another is a sacred
experience

Meeting at the soul
level, recognizing
the self in the other

Knowing and
feeling;

Affirming without
judgement; only
Loving

This is how lives
are changed and
how the world is
transformed.

Knowing the great
beauty to be found
in this world, yet
also knowing the
immense pain and
suffering;

Two parts of the
whole

Resting in the
assurance that
Love is the power
that heals the pain,
and reveals the
Beauty.

Open the eyes of
your heart to the
other

See the pain
behind masks of
anger, of cruelty,
of hatred.

Offer the gift of
your knowing and
allow healing,
however gradual,

To come.

Kiss the morning
hello, for this is the
day

You are invited to

BE LOVE in the
world...

Gratitude in a
most radical act

As it makes no
distinction
between

Plenty and want;

Health and ill;

Darkness and
light.

It sees only the
totality of Life,

The Gift of untold
value.

What if you, in all
of your so-called
brokenness,
weakness,
sinfulness and all,
were to come to
the realization
that you are
actually a perfect
manifestation of
The One Love
who created you?

Would that change
anything? Or,
would that change
everything?

On those God-
forsaken days
when your
strength is almost
gone, be kind, be
patient, be Love

To the you who is
doing your best to
keep going amidst
the onslaught of
emotions and
thoughts meant to
destroy the soul.

A new day will
come, bringing
with it relief and
renewal...

The mind is a liar

But the Soul is
where Truth
resides.

Take refuge there

Live from there

And your life will
become your own.

Fear is false

Love is the only
Truth

Your soul knows
this deeply

Believe it, embody
it, and bear
witness to
miracles.

*Look upon all that
surrounds you
with the eyes of
the heart*

*And find
nourishment for
your soul...*

Hidden pain

Unseen by others,
even from the self

Until it renders
you utterly
helpless

Can only be
unearthed by Love

To be revealed and
healed by The
Light...

*The warming and
softening of the
heart happens
gradually*

*Once you begin to
see yourself and
others through the
Lens of Truth ...*

*That we are all
created by Love
and we are all
One.*

The agonizing and
unending dry
spells in life are
sacred;

For the heart
needs them

To prepare for the
blessings to come,

When the soul find
its voice...

Self-imposed
isolation; alone in
my guilt and
shame

Unable to share
the depth of pain

Screaming for
relief, praying,
waiting...

Until, in a
moment, The Light
comes and I am
again connected to
Source

No longer hidden
away...

*From Whom all
blessings flow*

*The Source and
Spirit of Love*

*All gratitude flows
back in response*

*Out of the
awakened heart...*

The deep silence of
this new morning

Echoes the stillness
of my soul, as I
ready myself for
all that may come

And am reminded
once again,

All is well...

The new day
welcomes me

With open arms
and sky

Inviting me to

Love strongly

Shine brightly

And live deeply...

The night sky
offers mysteries

Gaze into the
expanse and know
that

You, too, are a
part of this vast
unknown...

There is no
pinnacle

There is only
process

Blessings abound

When you are
fully awake to Life.

*Dark, dense pain,
so deep, you can
sometimes only
hurt others in
response; but the
Light, if allowed,
obliterates the
dark. Find it,
stand in it; breathe
the Light and
nourish yourself
with it. Pain is
transformed into
Blessing; see
yourself as the
Light and take up
the Holy Journey.*

Self-knowledge is not gained by thinking;

It is found only by reflection with the heart.

Angels abound in
our world,

Though it might
not appear to be
so;

They are always
found when seen

Through the eyes
of Love.

The outside world,
encased in ice

Not unlike the
lonely heart, cold
and hard;

Until Source shines
Its Light

And the heart
warms with Truth.

At those moments
when distorted
reality sets in,
with all of its
challenges that
cannot be ignored,
circumstances that
cannot be changed;

I cry out to Spirit
in desperation

Then Grace visits
me with new
possibilities and
epiphanies, and I
am renewed by
hope and freedom.

Once again, my
eyes are open to
the almost
incomprehensible
beauty of all that
surrounds me;

Silent words of
gratitude to the
Source flow forth

From my soul.

Spirit tells me to
trust, but the fear
of error is almost
overwhelming;

Self steps aside as I
bow to the
unknown;

My mind quiets

My heart opens

And the adventure
that is life goes on.

Is the voice of the
soul falling silent?

Is the spark of
creativity
sputtering out?

Why do I feel so
dull and dry?

Source and Spirit
of Love, fill me
again with your
Truth

So that I can fully
live now, and in
the days to come...

I can feel
something dark
and familiar rising
from the depths,
and I am afraid;

Then, Beauty
comes to claim it;

Fear vanishes

And only Love
remains.

I am One who knows, says the Soul

I am One who weeps

I am One who sings

I am One who listens

I am One who prays;

For I am You...

Spirit conspires to
show the beauty
contained in all;

Open your eyes

Open your heart

You will find gifts
unimaginable;

Allow the world to
reveal the Love

Longing to be seen.

Wherever Truth,

Beauty,

Love,

or Courage are

made manifest,

There, Spirit
dwells.

When darkness
comes

Call on the Spirit
of Love

To lift the heavy
veil;

Almost invisible,
tiny sparks of
Light begin to
appear

And you start to
glow from within,

Illuminating the path
you travel.

The
transformation
miracle does not
come easily or
with haste;

Effort, time and
intention are all
needed; it is never
complete, but
brings us ever
closer to our true
selves, moment by
moment, joy to joy;

Until peace
overtakes the soul
and we rest in the
Fullness of Love.

Pain, confusion,
chaos; all around
me seems full of
unrest; when will
it end?

How can I stand
the unknowing?

Spirit tells me to
embrace the
mystery and "be
still and know"

Mind and soul
quiet as I relax
into life and learn
to trust...

Take your fear
and doubt out
from where they
reside

Speak them and let
them be known

Then, return to the
silent space that
Peace calls Home

And, find your
shelter there.

My heart has been
broken open

By the Beauty

Within, Without

And Eternal.

Made in the USA
Middletown, DE
28 February 2021